Ul

15 Key Steps to Un-Problem Your Problem

Problems are a part of life that we all encounter. No one can completely eliminate them, not even this book. However, if you've chosen to read this book with the goal of learning how to address and navigate your challenges effectively, you're on the right track.

This book will guide you in re-evaluating your problems, transforming what appears to be mysterious, keeps you stuck, or feels impossible to deal with into clear solutions. Along with the essential tools you'll acquire, this newfound clarity will empower you and enhance your ability to tackle challenges that once left you feeling defeated or overwhelmed.

In this book you will learn to:

- Make challenging relationships less challenging
- Take personal responsibility for the problem – and therefore be able to overcome it
- Communicate clearly to understand and be understood
- And so much more

If you're prepared to seize control and resolve your problems, pick up a copy of this impactful Itty Bitty™ book today!

Your Amazing Itty Bitty™ Un-Problem Your Problem Book

15 Key Steps to Un-Problem Your Problem

Ana Del Castillo

Published by Itty Bitty™ Publishing
A subsidiary of S & P Productions, Inc.

Printed in the United States of America

Itty Bitty Publishing
311 Main Street, Suite D
El Segundo, CA 90245
(310) 640-8885

ISBN: 978-1-7322946-7-7

This book is dedicated to anyone who has ever felt their problems were too big to handle, too much to bear, or too hard to work through. I personally spent decades under the weight of my problems before learning to un-problem them. My hope is that this book lightens the load and helps you un-problem the problems in your life.

Special thanks to S.B.I. and ThinkHuman, whose work impacted this book, and to all the teachers, coaches, practitioners, and friends who believed in me, supported me, and taught me the many things I know and teach today.

Finally, this is dedicated to my partner, best friend, and dear husband Ken. You have un-problemed many of my problems just by seeing and loving me deeply. I am so lucky to call you mine.

Truly, only you Ken Blackman. Only you.

Stop by our Itty Bitty™ website to find interesting blog entries to un-problem your problem.

www.IttyBittyPublishing.com

Or visit Ana Del Castillo at:

MyRightness.com

Table of Contents

Introduction

Everyone has problems. Some of us have worse problems, and others have great problems. But like taxes and death, problems are inevitable.

If you found this book hoping it will make all your problems disappear, I'll save you some time and tell you upfront that no one can make all your problems disappear. Not even this book.

But if you picked up this book with a desire to learn how to un-problem your problems, you've come to the right place. Here you will learn to *re*-see your problems so that what seemed mysterious, stuck, or impossible suddenly becomes clearer.

Clarity, coupled with other important tools you'll learn, will help you feel capable, skillful, and empowered to handle problems that used to make you feel defeated and ineffective.

One of my main goals in life is to have *great* problems, along the lines of, "Hey! I have an extra $100K. How should I spend it?"

Or, “I’ve never been this happy or joyful in my life! How do I take it all in?”

These are great problems to have.

If this is also a goal you’d like to have, I invite you to come along and learn to un-problem your problems!

Step 1
Do You Really Want to Un-Problem Your Problems?

We all have the power to un-problem problems, but few have the discipline or the will to do so. Stubbornness and pride can keep you stuck on a treadmill going nowhere because you're convinced you're right and can't stand something or someone getting the final word. That won't work here.

There's no moving forward if you refuse to get off your treadmill. So, before you jump in, get honest. When it comes to your problem(s):

1. Do you value being right more than being happy? Oops yes sometimes
2. Do you love winning more than peace of mind? Not anymore
3. Are you unable or unwilling to consider other points of view? working on it
4. Do you believe that someone or something is always right or always wrong? Have a tendency to think this way
5. Are you inflexible to the point that you're not open to alternative solutions to your problem? sometimes

More About Do You Really Want to Un-Problem Your Problems?

Wherever you are in your relationship with your problem, you selected this book because you want a breakthrough, or there's something you want to learn, shift, or change. So, to get the most out of this book, here are a few rules of play:

- **Decide** – Choose *now* to un-problem your problem. You don't need to know how, but you do need to decide you're going to do so.
- **Be willing** – Your life will greatly benefit from your willingness to get off the treadmill of being stuck in your problem.
- **Enthusiasm** – Get excited about learning how to escape the shackles of your problem.
- **Determination** – This takes commitment and practice. If you set your mind to it you can and will un-problem your problem.
- **Worthiness** – You and your happiness are worth more than your need to win at all costs.
- **Openness** – There are other ways to look at things. Be open to alternatives.

"Would you rather be right or free?"
- Byron Katie

Step 2
What's the Problem?

The first step to un-problem your problem is to write things down—everything from work, school, social obligations, and everything in between. Pour out all your problems and go into the whole story! If you're not sure how to begin, here are four approaches to try.

1. **Stream of consciousness** – Let your brain spill out. Pour out your thoughts, however mundane, on paper for at least 15 minutes without stopping.
2. **Question and answer** – If stream of consciousness feels too overwhelming, ask yourself questions, i.e., "How do I feel about this?" or, "What's the biggest issue I have with it?" Then answer the question.
3. **Mind map** – If you aren't into writing or you're a visual thinker, try the following: mind mapping[1]. Start with a single word at the center, like "family" or "finances," and map it out from there.
4. **Numbers** – If you think practically, write out your problem in Excel with numbers, dates, and times.

[1] https://en.wikipedia.org/wiki/Mind_map

Why Do I Ask You to Write Down Your Problems?

If you've ever found yourself going over the same problem in your head again and again, writing will help you with the following.

- **Stress relief** – In itself, the act of writing clears your mind and helps lessen the time spent thinking about the problem.
- **Creativity** – Studies have shown[2] writing increases creativity and deepens your thinking to help you think outside the box.
- **Feelings** – Writing about feelings improves your mood to help flesh out your thoughts in an orderly manner to lighten your burdens.
- **Perspective** – Writing your thoughts allows you to see them from a different perspective, compared to replaying them in your mind. This can reveal something helpful you hadn't seen before.
- **Faster Processing** – It has been shown[3] that writing helps you overcome tough moments faster.

So, start writing!

---

[2] https://www.sparringmind.com/benefits-of-writing/
[3] https://hbr.org/2021/07/writing-can-help-us-heal-from-trauma

Step 3
You've Got All These Problems! Now What?

Since most problems don't go away until you deal with them, in this step you start the powerful process of dealing with problems and learning to un-problem them, too! Using the writing exercise in Step 2, choose one problem you wish to un-problem. You may have several, but for now just choose one to tackle.

Take a clean sheet of paper. At the top of the page, reduce the issue to one sentence. Examples:

1. I don't have enough money to pay my bills.
2. My boss belittles me.
3. I can't seem to lose weight.
4. My parents don't understand me or support my choices.
5. My wife won't have sex with me.

Underneath the sentence, write down your beliefs about the problem. Examples:

1. It's hopeless.
2. There's nothing I can do about it.
3. Things will never change; it's doomed/I'm doomed.
4. Life isn't fair.

Illuminating Your Context: The Problem Behind Your Problem

Your context is the background stuff contributing to and supporting your problem. Understanding how your context feeds and props up your problem is important for the following reasons.

- **Interpretation** – Your background context provides overlooked information that helps you better understand the actions and events in your problem.
- **Communication** – Becoming aware of your background context enables you to adapt communication and messages to better address the situation.
- **Understanding** – Better comprehension of the contextual background of the situation or people involved helps you better understand *their* perspective, which in turn gives you more power.
- **Decision-making** – A fuller context helps you identify factors and constraints that may not be immediately apparent, but will lead to more creative and effective solutions.

Step 4
The Problem Influencing Your Problem

To un-problem your problem, digging deeper up-front at the beliefs influencing the problem will yield powerful results later. On the same piece of paper, write down your beliefs about the other person, organization, or group. Try to narrow each belief down to one sentence. Examples:

1. They're a lazy POS!
2. She's a disgusting liar.
3. My job is toxic and sexist.
4. He's a selfish $!&*% who only cares about himself.

Below those beliefs write down your beliefs about yourself. Again, narrow each belief down to one sentence. Examples:

1. I'm such a failure; I can't do anything right.
2. Nobody likes me; I'm too annoying and uninteresting.
3. I'm too old/fat/ugly; no one will ever find me attractive.
4. I'm not smart enough/good enough.

Be as Truthful and Authentic as You Can

- The more honest you are, the more breakthroughs you'll have.
- No one will see this except you, so don't be afraid to let it rip.
- Embrace your beliefs and feelings rather than suppress them. This will pave the way for better feelings about yourself and better relationships with others.

If you think people are evil, don't shy away from it. If you believe you're stupid, write it down, but not because it's true! Do it because:

- It's important to take an honest look at what's in the background unconsciously influencing your problem. This will powerfully assist to un-problem your problem.
- Being honest will help you make better decisions based on facts rather than distorted perceptions.
- Being honest with yourself and your beliefs empowers you when confronting challenges. It shows you where you can make powerful changes to un-problem your problem and influence your situation for the better.

Step 5
Are You Part of Your Problem?

Quantum physics provides a great metaphor for how we're all deeply interconnected, how thoughts are the source of reality, and how everything we experience is a product of thought energy. What does that have to do with you and your problem? Everything!

1. Go back to your notes and look at all your assumptions and beliefs.
2. Consider how these background thoughts and beliefs influence the way you behave and act inside your problem.
3. Write down all the ways you're acting within your problem due to your beliefs. Are you aloof? Angry? Insecure?

How do you think you act toward someone you believe is evil, stupid, or lazy? Do you think they can feel it even if you never say it? Consider the following:

1. Your beliefs and behavior directly shape your experiences and outcomes.
2. Your behavior may inadvertently create or perpetuate the very problems you aim to overcome.

Response Ability Is Power!

Realizing your influence and focusing on your "response ability" (your ability to choose your own responses) greatly increases your personal power and expands your scope of influence. In other words:

- Focus on how *you* influence things. This empowers you to find solutions or adapt to reduce the impact of the problem in your life.
- Focusing exclusively on what people or things do to you keeps *you* stuck and powerless.

Consider that how you interpret the world around you always aligns with your beliefs. Your behavior is directed by your interpretation, and consequences result from your behavior.

- If you believe that situations happen to you and there's nothing you can do to influence them this reduces your power, rendering you unable to make a difference.
- Believing you can influence things around you and then adjusting your response to possibly create a better situation makes you able to respond and adapt more effectively.

Step 6
It's Not Fair —*They're* the Problem!

At this point in the process, people usually dig their heels in and get stuck. I get it. Who wants to be responsible or let someone or something (God, the government, a competitor) off the hook?

1. Maybe someone has really done you dirty.
2. Maybe there's legitimate justification for treating them the way you are.
3. Maybe you're understandably upset and angry that responsibility has fallen on you when it's not your fault.

All those things may be true; it has certainly happened to me. But as much as I wish life were equitable and fair, it's not. And the truth is you opened this book because you want to un-problem your problem. So that means:

1. You need to consciously choose your power instead of choosing to be resentful and "right" about being wronged.
2. Becoming fiercely determined to reclaim your agency and rise above all obstacles.

You Have the Power to Change Your Story!

You are the author of your own story. With every action and decision you make, you acquire the ability to rewrite your narrative to shape it into the life you truly desire. By owning this you gain in several ways.

- **A sense of control** – By taking ownership of your story you reclaim your power and cease being the victim of circumstances.
- **Resiliency** – By learning to overcome your challenges you bounce back more quickly and gain a more positive outlook in life.
- **Self-esteem** – By writing your own story you align to your true being, not to whomever you feel resigned to be.

This is your opportunity to rise above the hurt, grow stronger, and regain control of your own destiny. It will:

- Improve your mental health and emotional well-being.
- Inspire you to take bold actions, push your limits, and become the best version of yourself. This ultimately leads to a more fulfilling and satisfying life.

Step 7
What if the Problem Is You Believe There's a Problem?

Now that you've recommitted to un-problem your problem, let's look at the very structure of what a problem is.

1. A problem is a situation or obstacle that hinders progress or prevents the achievement of a desired goal.
2. A problem means something or someone is "wrong." (I am wrong/you are wrong/life is wrong).
3. A problem means that someone has to be the problem (I am the problem/you are the problem/life is a problem). So to fix it you must combat, dominate, manipulate, calculate, control, coerce, etc.

That's a pretty powerless setup! Couple that with all the context you bring, and no wonder you feel stuck and ineffective. Here are a couple of ideas to consider:

1. What if your problem isn't really a problem?
2. What if you calling it a problem is part of the problem?

Create a Life Filled With Challenges, Not Problems

If a challenge is a demanding task you want to overcome, and a problem is something difficult to deal with or understand that impedes your progress, the key difference between the two is your attitude.

- Challenges require determination and adaptability, whereas problems encourage resignation and paralysis.
- Challenges are difficult tasks or situations that test your abilities. They're opportunities for your growth and improvement.

Most people view problems negatively. But approaching them as challenges with a positive outlook to overcome can shift your mindset in a game-changing way.

- It encourages curiosity, agency, choices, and options.
- It inspires personal responsibility and a more robust, honest approach to life.
- It builds pathways to personal power and will grow your ability to shift your circumstances.

Step 8
Great! You Got All These "Challenges," Now What?

Here's where you start to un-problem your problems in real time. To begin, consider that a problem is essentially an argument. Your goal is to shift from arguing to conversing. When it comes to arguments:

1. Misunderstandings, differing expectations, and clashing perspectives only lead to tension and conflict.
2. They escalate, making people hostile and aggressive until each person is focused on asserting dominance or proving a point.
3. They damage relationships and create negativity.

But challenges require you to master challenging conversations. This is where the magic happens! Challenging conversations:

1. Greatly enhance your problem-solving skills
2. Strengthen your relationships
3. Boost your confidence, helping to navigate complex situations with more ease

Mastering the Craft of Challenging Conversations Is a Superpower!

Eventually, we all face uncomfortable situations or topics with people we care about. But the difference between an argument and a challenging conversation is intention and skillset. Think about it. Both are interactions between two or more parties characterized by:

- Elevated emotional intensity
- Differing viewpoints
- Perceived high stakes for at least one party

However, there's a way to have challenging conversations with people that are civil and also productive. Remember:

- Everyone wants to be heard, even those we disagree with.
- You can build rapport, ask the right questions, and find points of agreement even when you disagree.

Every strong relationship is built on a foundation of challenging conversations.

Step 9
Why Are Challenging Conversations So Challenging?

If the words, "We need to talk," fill you with dread, you're not alone. Difficult conversations about topics such as money, sex, politics, religion, feelings (heck, almost everything) can be awkward and unpleasant. Common fears are:

1. Confrontation
2. Being disliked
3. Saying the wrong thing or making it worse
4. The other person's reaction

To make matters worse, two of the most important things needed to make challenging conversations successful—expressing emotion and listening—become compromised when you're activated, angry, or upset.

1. Strong emotions like anger, self-pity or sadness turn your focus inward.
2. Emotions such as sadness, anger, or personal dislike filter and color what you hear until it matches your mood.

There's a Scientific Reason Why These Conversations Are Challenging

According to neuroscientists, receiving feedback or criticism triggers the brain's threat response system in the amygdala, which is responsible for processing emotions like fear and anxiety.

- When the amygdala perceives a threat, it activates the fight-or-flight response.
- It releases stress hormones and increases heart rate and blood pressure.
- The threat response makes it difficult to think clearly, process information effectively, and respond constructively.

This isn't just true for you; it's true for everyone. Understanding neuroscience will help you have challenging conversations in a more constructive manner to reduce the threat response in others. Your biggest takeaways are:

- Receiving feedback and criticism triggers the brain's threat response system.
- Understanding this neurological process empowers you to use that information to create better understanding and collaboration.

Step 10
The Magic Key to Un-Problem Your Problem

It's now time for you to learn the most important distinction in this process. For a challenging conversation to go well, your intention must be generous. The person you have the problem with must be included in the "win" or positive net gain. If your intention is to tell them how stupid/ wrong/bad they are, or to punish or patronize them, don't bother to have the conversation. You'll end up creating more of what you already have, or worse.

What generous means here:

1. You want a better dynamic for both of you because your attitude or behavior toward them has changed for the worse.
2. You care, they matter, and if you don't speak up, things will remain the same or get worse.
3. You see a possibility for them they don't see for themselves, and you want to bring it to their awareness.

Your Generous Intention Is Your GPS

If you really want the dynamic to change, the magic is figuring out how to genuinely invest and care about them, then speaking and intending from there.

Examples of generous intention:

- "I think you're a very special/talented person and I'm invested in feeling that way even more. Can we talk about something I've noticed?"
- "I'd love to hear how you're doing, and I miss how close we used to be. Would you like to connect?"
- "We're partners and I trust you. There's something that's recently gotten in the way of that trust for me. Are you open to hearing about it?"

Examples of ungenerous intention:

- "You're selfish, and I've lost all respect for you. Start acting like a grown-up or else."
- "You don't care! I've asked you twenty times to ____ and you refuse to do it! What do I have to do to get through that thick, stupid, skull of yours?"
- "I care about you and only want what's best for you." (Only you don't care and you're manipulating for a different outcome.)

Step 11
A Framework to Un-Problem Your Problem

Now that you've written the name and subject of the problem, and you've come up with a generous intention, we're ready for the actual framework for your challenging conversation. Underneath your generous intention, briefly write the facts of the problem and the measurable observable behaviors or attitudes you want to address.[4] For example:

1. "Over the last three months, you've been consistently late to every morning workout."
2. "Whenever we talk about money (sex, family, having a child, etc.) we usually end up fighting."
3. "I've had a goal to change my diet, but for the last six months, I haven't changed. In fact, my weight is climbing."
4. "I haven't been able to keep up with my bills and my debt is growing."
5. "Lately, whenever I try to connect with you, you've got other plans."
6. "I've noticed how often you tell me what you're unhappy about and it seems more pronounced lately."

[4] https://think-human.com/

It's Important to Separate Data and Facts From Your Story and Interpretation of Facts

I promise that your story and interpretation—your experience—will come into play and be expressed. However, to offset the way our brains default to threat, only refer to data points and facts in a way that acknowledges the landscape and issues without extraneous concerns.

- Pay attention if you add interpretation or opinion to your data and facts.
- There's a difference between saying, "I've noticed how often you tell me you're unhappy," and, "You're always criticizing me."
- This method also applies to discussions or issues you have with yourself.

Generous intention coupled with straight data and facts does the following:

- Builds credibility
- Encourages open discussions
- Reduces potential conflicts
- Fosters more common ground
- Creates empathy, willingness, understanding
- Supports objective discussions

Step 12
Naming the Impact

This is where you express how the issue impacts you, their reputation or others', your relationship with them, etc. Examples:

1. "You've consistently been late to almost every workout. I've felt frustrated, leaving me with the impression that you don't care, or worse, you're lazy."
2. "… we usually end up fighting. When you walk out or threaten the relationship, I feel hopeless and afraid; I have the feeling you're insensitive or a jerk."
3. "… in fact, my weight is climbing. It feels like you don't listen; I feel powerless, enraged, like there's something wrong with us."
4. "… my debt is growing. Each time I speak up, I'm shoved down, not listened to or respected. I'm starting to hate you for it."
5. "… it seems to be more pronounced lately. It feels like I can't win; it makes me want to give up in anger."

How You Couch the Impact Matters

Remember that you spent time in Step 2 writing out the story of your problem. And in Step 5, you discovered that your unconscious context and your behavior was partially creating the dynamic and stuck-ness of your problem.

In this step, you essentially do the same thing for them. You show them how their behavior has a deleterious effect on you, themselves, their lives, relationships, etc. Your goals are:

- Staying focused on your true north. You bring this up because you want something better for them, and in turn for you.
- Bypassing the default defenses in your brain and their brain to take things personally and feel threatened.
- Doing these things with understanding, patience and compassion.

Step 13
Personal Responsibility and Requests

This is where all the work in Step 5 is used to your advantage and you take responsibility for your side of the equation. Taking personal responsibility:

1. Diffuses tension and demonstrates emotional maturity
2. Shows empathy for the other person's perspective, promotes mutual respect and understanding, and fosters conflict resolution
3. Focuses on the issue at hand without assigning blame, which leads to quicker resolutions

What personal responsibility do you have right now for the issue at hand? Could you have said something sooner? Did you assume things? Here are examples:

1. "I've felt frustrated, leaving me with the impression you're lazy or you don't care. To be honest, I should have said something sooner before resentment set in."
2. "I feel like I can't win, and it makes me want to give up in anger. My attitude has exacerbated things."

Personal Responsibility Paves the Way to Make a Request

This is your opportunity to make a request, which is the reason you're doing it in the first place. You want something to be different! This is your chance to ask for what you want. What is your request? If you could wave a magic wand, what would change? Keep in mind that a great request has the following criteria.

- **Clear and specific** – The most effective requests clearly state the desired outcome or action so there's no misunderstanding.
- **Thoughtful and respectful** – Thoughtful acknowledgment for the other party makes the request easier to hear and increases the likelihood of a positive response.
- **Timely and urgent** – A deadline helps set expectations and allows the other party to prioritize accordingly.

For example: "…before my resentment set in. Now that I'm speaking up, my request and what I'd love is for you to show up on time starting Monday next week."

Step 14
Opening the Dialogue and Active Listening

The next step in this framework is to invite a conversation! All your preparation, (separating story from fact, generous intention, stating the issue succinctly, sharing the impact, and making a request), all serve to ground and open the actual conversation.

Once you've shared your thoughts:

1. Open the dialogue to understand their perspective and experience.
2. Be curious. Ask at least three questions and avoid solving things right away to make sure you fully resolve the issue.
3. Once you really understand them, their perspective and their world, reaffirm your intention and then collaboratively come up with solutions or next steps.

This is a conversation, not an argument.

1. Keep the conversation on track by referring to your generous intention.
2. Avoid unrelated past issues or grievances.

Engage in Active Listening to Create an Exquisite Connection

Active listening is like a magical empathy potion. It helps you better understand the speaker's feelings, needs, and perspectives. Suddenly you're not just waiting to make your point, you're an empathetic human being listening actively! Active listening means:

- You fully focus, comprehend, and respond to a speaker.
- You demonstrate genuine interest and engagement in the conversation.
- You pay attention to verbal and non-verbal cues.
- You ask clarifying questions.
- You provide feedback or paraphrase to confirm you understand the other side.

Annoying misunderstandings can make life miserable. They can vanish when you actively listen, enabling you to grasp the true meaning behind words to avoid petty conflicts.

Active listening helps you bond with others and create genuine connections, making your relationships stronger. It supports you in identifying issues, finding solutions, and makes your world a better place.

To create magic, start with, “What are your thoughts?” and then listen actively and attentively.

Step 15
You Now Have the Tools to Un-Problem Your Problems!

Congratulations, you made it! You have the tools, steps, and know-how to un-problem your problems.

Here's a recap and review of the steps to un-problem your problems:

1. Write down all your problems, pick one problem, and reduce it to a one-word description.
2. Illuminate the context of your problem by writing down all your beliefs about the person or subject. Then write your larger beliefs about yourself or life in this problem.
3. Take a sober, responsible look at how your context influences your behavior and co-creates your problem.
4. Create a generous intention for your challenging conversation.
5. Follow the framework: state your generous intention, describe the facts, name the impact, take responsibility, make a request, open the dialogue, and listen actively![5]

[5] https://think-human.com/

The Time to Un-Problem Your Problems is NOW

It's true that not every problem will un-problem or resolve itself the way you want or hope. Let go of your expectations, accept reality as it is, and make empowered decisions from there. This reduces your disappointment and frustration, which in itself un-problems your problem.

- Have courage, jump in, get comfortable and masterful with the discomfort of challenge, and watch your relationships and your life improve with each problem you commit to un-problem.
- And if you're excited about getting started but feel like you'd like some extra support, don't fret! Lots of people feel this way starting out. There are solutions for whatever anxieties you may feel, and there are helpful resources and support at your fingertips!

For a workbook to support you to un-problem your problem, register for a group workshop to un-problem your problem, or for more direct support, go to: myrightness.com.

You've finished. Before you go…

Post/Share that you finished this book.

Please star rate this book.

Reviews are solid gold to writers. Please take a few minutes to give us some itty bitty feedback.

ABOUT THE AUTHOR

Ana Del Castillo is a Cuban Middle-Eastern Jewish woman in her fifties who laughs loudly, gives full-body hugs, and grew up debating—a normal mode of everyday conversation.

She is married to Ken Blackman, the love of her life and often feels like she won the lottery as life wasn't always this good. Her childhood was filled with violence and sexual trauma starting at the age of 5. At 21 she left home to follow her dream and become a successful Broadway actress and singer.

Tragically, she then lost her father and brother in a brutal gangland-style killing. After that, she spent over 30 years making herself whole through extraordinary determination and commitment.

Today, her day job is writing, speaking, and helping to "Sherpa" women through emotional and psychological issues so they too can feel "right" about themselves. Her passion and expertise is women, personal freedom and power. Ana is a certified coach and a women's rightness expert.

For Ana, "rightness" is the cultivated freedom and power of a quiet brain and emotional body at peace. It means being comfortable in your skin, your sex, your anger, your grief, your joy and your life. And it definitely means not apologizing or feeling ashamed about who you are.

She passionately believes that being less than your full authentic self is an act against nature. In a world where women are constantly told they are simultaneously too much and not enough, being unabashedly and authentically themselves is an act of revolution.

Her life's work is that revolution.

Ana has spoken to audiences all over the country and has coached female rock stars, entrepreneurs, and homemakers about the power and freedom of authentic rightness. She has been featured on *National Public Radio, New York Post, People Magazine, Shout Out LA,* and *The Moth.*

For more information, visit myrightness.com.

If you enjoyed this Itty Bitty™ book you might also like…

- **Your Amazing Itty Bitty™ Conscious Co-Creation Book** by Heidi Katara Funk

- **Your Amazing Itty Bitty™ Relationships as a Spiritual Practice** by Deborah A. Gayle

- **Your Amazing Itty Bitty™ Grief Book** by Lisa Y. Herrington

Or any of the many Amazing Itty Bitty™ books available online at www.ittybittypublishing.com

Made in the USA
Las Vegas, NV
21 July 2024